Rookie Read-About™ Science

# How Do You Know It's Fall?

By Allan Fowler

**Consultants:**

Robert L. Hillerich, Ph.D., Bowling Green
State University, Bowling Green, Ohio

Mary Nalbandian, Director of Science,
Chicago Public Schools, Chicago, Illinois

Fay Robinson, Child Development Specialist

CHILDRENS PRESS ®

CHICAGO

Design by Beth Herman Design Associates

## Library of Congress Cataloging-in-Publication Data

Fowler, Allan
  How do you know it's fall? / by Allan Fowler.
    p.  cm. –(Rookie read-about science)
  Summary: Presents the many signs of fall, including geese flying south,
squirrels hiding acorns, and people playing football.
  ISBN 0-516-14922-4
  1. Autumn–Juvenile literature. [1. Autumn.] I. Title. II. Series: Fowler, Allan.
  Rookie read-about science.
QB637.7.F69 1992                                                91-35060
508–dc20                                                              CIP
                                                                         AC

How do you know it's fall?

When the green leaves of summer turn red or yellow or brown and they fall off the trees...

when you look up and
see flocks of geese or
other birds flying to a
warmer place...

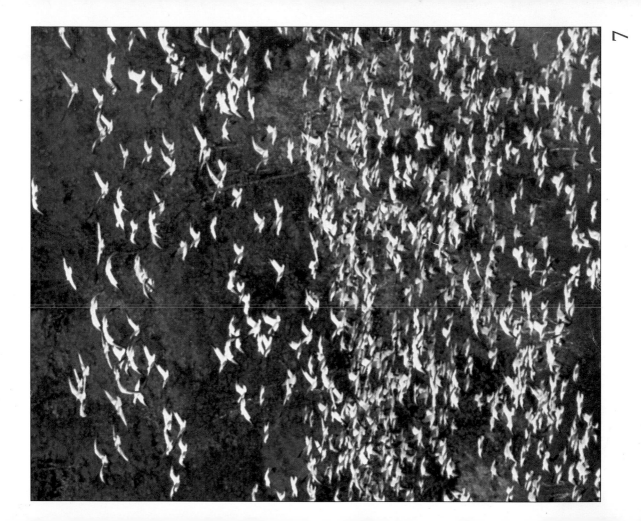

when you're back in school

telling your friends what
you did last summer...

when some days are so
chilly that you need a
jacket...

then you know it's fall!

Farmers work hard in the fall. They reap their corn, harvest their potatoes,

and pick ripe fruit off trees.

Squirrels know that winter is not far off.

They gather acorns or nuts and hide them to eat later.

Halloween comes in the fall...

and pumpkins with funny faces smile at you.

Later in the fall, everyone in the family sits down to a big Thanksgiving feast.

Fall is football time.

People watch games and
cheer for their team.

A crisp, clear fall day is a wonderful time for playing outdoors.

As the days become
cooler and cooler...
it gets dark earlier
and earlier.

Why is the season called fall?

Because it's the time of year when leaves fall. Another name for fall is autumn.

Many people make special trips just to see the beautiful fall colors.

You are very lucky if you live in a place where leaves change color in the fall.

# Words You Know

potatoes

corn

autumn

fall

leaves

football

Halloween
pumpkins

Thanksgiving

# Index

## About the Author

Allan Fowler is a free-lance writer with a background in advertising. Born in New York, he lives in Chicago now and enjoys traveling.

## Photo Credits

PhotoEdit – ©Tony Freeman, 8, 18, 31, (bottom left); ©Mary Kate Denny, 9; ©Myrleen Ferguson, 16, 23; ©Ron Grishaber, 17, 31 (bottom right); John Neubauer, 30 (bottom right)

Valan – ©Kennon Cooke, Cover, 14, 25; ©Irwin Barrett, 5, 30 (top right); ©Francis Lepine, 7; ©Ian Davis-Young, 11; ©Guy Lebel, 12, 30 (bottom left); ©Phillip Norton, 13; ©Robert C. Simpson, 20, 31 (top); ©V. Whelan, 26; ©Joseph R. Pearce, 29, 30 (top left)

COVER: Grey squirrel